Div-Tieflings

A Roleplaying Game Supplement

By Anthony Uyl

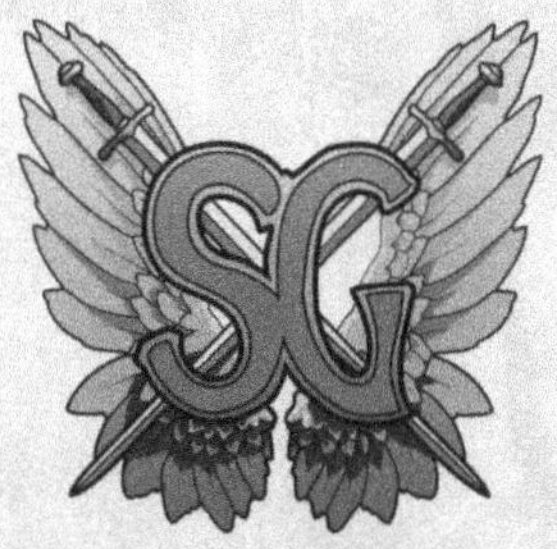

Ingersoll, Ontario, Canada 2021

Div-Tieflings

A Roleplaying Game Supplement

Written by Anthony Uyl

Artwork by Christopher Cortright

Cover and interior background designs done by Lord Zsezse Works

See page 31 and 32 for Product Identity and Open Gaming Content information.

What kind of stories do you have? Let us know!

Visit our Facebook page: @solacegames
Follow us on Twitter: @solacegamesrpg
Contact us at: solacegames@hotmail.com
See the full catalogue of Devoted Publishing and Solace Games books at:
http://www.lulu.com/spotlight/devotedpublishing

Published in Ingersoll, Ontario, Canada 2021

ISBN: 978-1-77356-420-3

Table of Contents

Introduction

Whenever I go to conventions and customers search through the pile of miniatures that I have for sale, the question always comes up: "do you have any Tieflings?" For some reason I am always surprised by this. Mainly the surprise comes from the wide popularity of Tieflings among gamers. I am not sure what it is about them that makes them so popular, but nevertheless, people are always fascinated by these infernal children.

While doing research for this book, I admit some of the curiosity peaked for me as well. When delving into lore and other sources of information for this type of people group, you really can find an interesting bit of history and text to use in any kind of gaming environment. While I had never heard of the Div before, I found myself eagerly sorting through different books and websites to learn more about the history of these spirits.

Doing all this work, I hope I have been able to pay proper respect and homage to the lore that I dug up. While it is not always possible to one-hundred-percent portray a creature of this type in its proper historical context, my hope for you is that you find joy in playing a Div-Tiefling and that your curiosity, like mine, can be piqued. Hopefully, you are able to learn something as I have.

President/Owner Solace Games
Anthony Uyl

Chapter I - Div-Tieflings

Αστειος Διαβολος (Asteios Diabolos; Beautiful Devil)

Coming from a strange parentage of demonic creatures that typically roam in desert places, many are shocked by the charm and beauty that often accompanies the Div-Tieflings. Many have seen the demonic beings that infest this bloodline and all attest that the physical charm that comes from them is surprising. The Div themselves are hideous and grotesque, often turning wanderers away simply by looking at them. Their warlike nature however is present in Div-Tieflings and the strength these people have shown is an evident testimony to their desire to dominate all life.

Many have attained great positions of grandeur both financially and as warlords. Where strength rules, these Tieflings have always found a home. They are drawn to strife like a moth to flame, they cannot avoid it. Their parentage makes this obvious as a non-fighting Div-Tiefling is often seen with suspicion. They are known by their need and desire for violence, if one is living peacefully, there is usually some game being played. It is only a matter of time until they lash out and kill people around them.

Those Div-Tieflings that are troubled by their violent heritage have been known to join monasteries to try and subdue their heritage through meditation and acts of contrition. Others have taken to walking the desert and lonely places of the world as guardians protecting those that are attacked by bandits. Many have found a home in the lonely places of the world, but still at some point a breaking point comes upon them and they must for some inner reason, perform an act of violence.

How long these people have been around is hard to determine. They have always seemed to come up through a parentage often without any knowledge of their Div nature. Many parents are surprised when these children are born, as the lineage they come from has nothing to do with desert parentage. Many of these families have forgotten their bloodline and continued in life without any thought of it. The blood does not forget however, and eventually the dominant part of their blood comes to the fore and gives birth to what many parents consider abominations and bad omens.

There are those that have tried to find a place for these Tieflings in society. As children they are usually trained as warriors to lead armies for great and evil kings. While the Div-Tieflings do not realize to what end they are being used, many of them give in easily to this deception, as violence is all they would know apart from their patron anyway. Others are taken into slavery in some way, usually in pleasure houses for their great beauty. Many nobles have secretly paid great amounts of money to spend a night with a Div-Tiefling. Many have tried to claim these acts as some badge of honour.

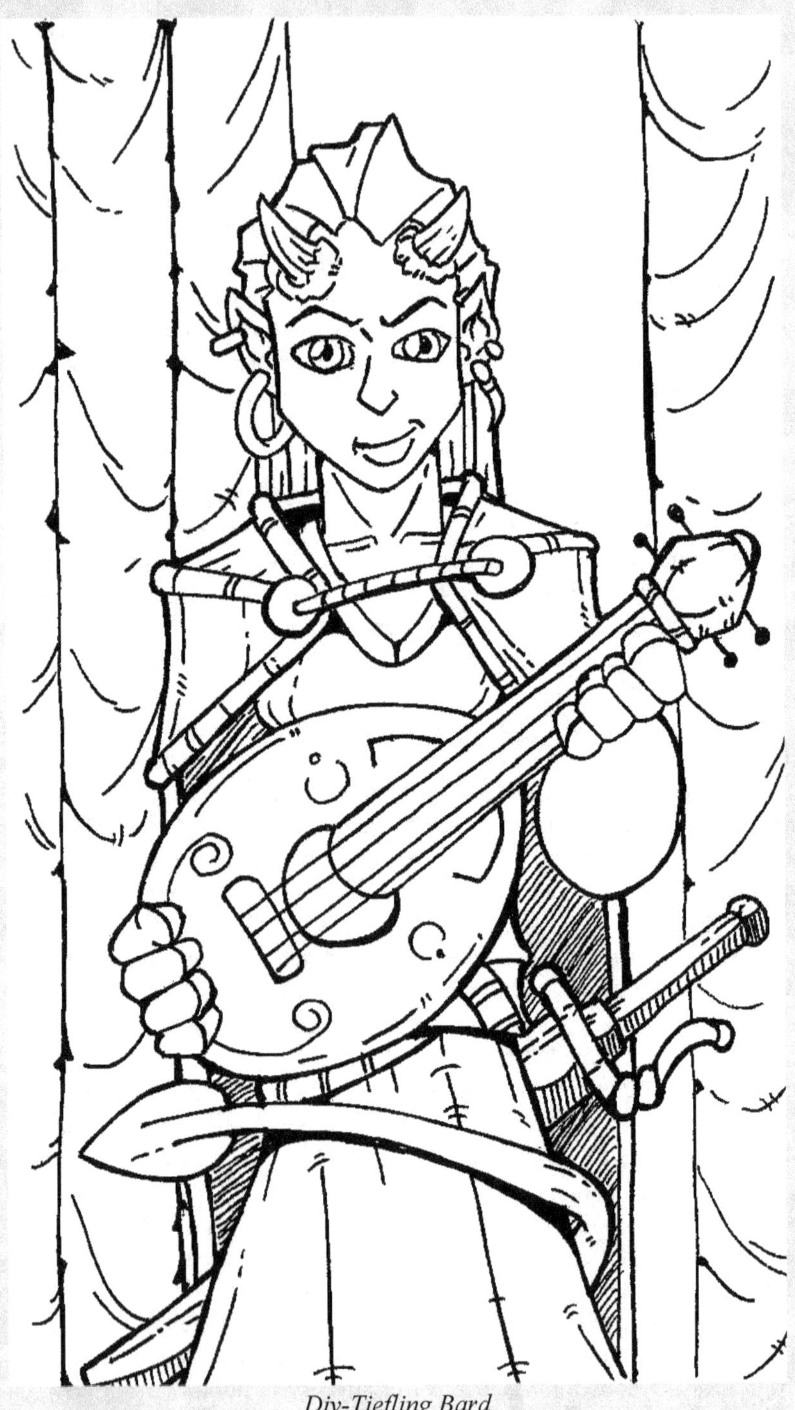

Div-Tiefling Bard

Truth be told, all these acts are dangerous to begin with. These Tieflings have been known to turn on their oppressors and many times taking over the kingdom or pleasure house to their own whims. These kingdoms and houses then become dens of evil and treachery as the Div-Tiefling takes their demonic nature out on those around them. They will stop at nothing to dominate others. Some will do so with as little violence as possible, while others spill as much blood as they can in the act. Regardless of the amount of violence used, there is always violence to be had when a Div-Tiefling is involved.

Physical Description

It is difficult to determine just how exactly any two Div-Tieflings will look when compared together. They come in all kinds of heights, skin colours and cultural traits. Neither parents, mother nor father, has more influence genetically as to what exactly these Tieflings will look like. All that can be determined when a child is born about their parentage is the long slender tail, horns on their heads and the ethereal beauty that enraptures the child.

As was mentioned, Div-Tieflings come in all skin colours. Some are dark skinned while others are lighter. Their desert parentage does not seem to have any determination as to what their colouring may be. The lighter the skin colour however, the more devilish the child will look with blue, red or any other colour veins spreading all over their skin. Despite their skin colour, Div-Tiefling hair is always of bright and vibrant colours. Some of their hair is red, purple or blue. Others are highly possible and likely.

Society

There is no definite society of gathered Div-Tieflings. For the most part it simply has never been attempted because of the dominating personality traits that these people all possess. Also, to note, is that Div-Tieflings will usually try to dominate any community that they are in. These communities can vary from a local pub to an entire city-state. Many people have tried to enslave them, but this has never turned out well for the enslavers.

Where these Tieflings have found an accepted role in society, they are usually set up as commanders of armies and institutions. They are brilliant leaders and those that use them in this role also carefully watch them for instances of cold-blooded murder. Non-Div-Tiefling leaders recognize the violent nature of these people and so try to settle the violent urges but this is not always achievable. Other societies have also attempted to let them fight in gladiator rings to try and get them to quell the aggressive tendencies of the Div bloodline.

The use of magic is rare within the social constructs of the Div-Tieflings. While they recognize that there is a supernatural world out there for them to manipulate, they simply prefer not to do so. Div-Tieflings prefer the coldness of steel over the "treachery" of magic. This does not mean that all these people have completely rejected the use of magic, some have become quite accomplished spell casters. The majority just prefer to go into situations with what they can see and touch, not what they can summon forth. There seems to be more surety in that for them and any other belief in magic is often seen as "superstitious" rather than based in fact.

Relations

Other races usually look with suspicion upon the Div-Tieflings. Many of these other peoples have discovered how these Tieflings desire to take over any operation or kingdom in the cruelest of ways. This does not mean that every community will immediately turn them away, some of the more sinister or desperate settlements will gladly take these people in to attempt to gain some stability or an upper hand against a foe that has been harassing them.

Those communities that are fully aware of what these Tieflings are capable of will quickly try to come to terms of peace with any that are at the forefront of an attack army. Their cruelty is legendary, and no one is interested in having them loot and sack their homes. This has caused some towns to take them in despite what they suspect will inevitably happen. These towns simply do not want these Div-Tieflings to go somewhere else and come back leading an attack force that will wipe them from the map.

Alignment and Religion

Div-Tieflings are very apt to take after their infernal heritage in their ways of beliefs. Many of these people have no clue just which Div is truly their parent, but they strive to find out with great diligence. It is strange that a child of infernal descent would take a neutral stance, while still maintaining an air of evil. They have tried not to take sides in the great debate between law and chaos but are vigilant in their general ideas of evil. This does not mean there are not good or truly neutral Tieflings. There are in fact quite a few, but most of them have chosen to take a more insidious path. Those that are good are often seen as outcasts by their own kind. This forces even those evil Div-Tieflings that are viewed with suspicion to hold the good aligned Tieflings almost in exile.

For a group of people that have literally been bred of evil, it is surprising to find that the belief in the gods seems to be a dividing theme among them. Some have taken to paths of faith quite vigilantly, seeking out gods from all walks of life to follow and give devotion to, others have strived to divine who their Div parent is to give them the worship the Tiefling feels they deserve. While these people have aptitudes for evil, some have willingly desired the power of gods and devils to further their ambitions. Those that follow these paths have become greatly renown magic-users and prophets.

There are those that have for the most part spurned practical religion in the favour of agnosticism. They believe that the gods are best left alone and left as unknown entities. Some of these more military based Div-Tieflings will sometimes still give devotion to a god or infernal deity, but this is more lip-service then actual piety. Those in this way of thinking are commonly criticizing those that give wholehearted devotion to the divine, but they still realize there is power that is best left alone that their devoted brothers have somehow gained access to.

Table: Typical Div Infernal Lords

Deity	Alignment	Suggested Domains	Symbol
Amitos	NE	Trickery	glove and dagger
Chalmek	LE	War	sword with eyes
Chemosh	CE	Death	goblet of blood
Lartoi	NE	Nature	tree of shadows
Memsal	NE	Tempest	trident in the sea
Orgol	CE	Death, War	kneeling demon
Yktat	LE	Knowledge	book with blood stain
Z'zbip	NE	Nature, Tempest	rock dripping water

Overview of the Typical Div Infernal Lords

Amitos. A devious Div that tries to advance her infernal goals with subterfuge and lies. Many others of her kind distrust her but rely on her and her followers to get information that they cannot obtain normally. Followers of Amitos stick to the shadows professionally but live the high life otherwise.

Chalmek. A bloodthirsty infernal, Chalmek will stop at nothing to prove his dominance over all mortal and immortal life. Nothing gives him greater joy than to shed the blood of his enemies and to bathe in the gore afterwards. Many other infernal Div have preferred to avoid Chalmek at all costs.

Chemosh. A Div that waits in the shadows and awaits the coming souls of fallen Div-Tieflings. While he would like to judge over all souls of all mortals that cross the plane of death, Chemosh only sits in judgment over the Div-Tieflings that meet the unfortunate results of death.

Lartoi. A female Div that rules over the untamed realms of nature. She despises anything that has to do with the urban environment. She desires for nature to take back the land at any cost. Many have come under her sway and demanded that the Div-Tieflings that take up urban dwellings be named heretics.

Memsal. This devious Div loves to torment ships at sea. She will cause any ship and its crew to undergo the most vicious of storms until they give her tribute. More times than not, this tribute is a blood sacrifice. If the crew refuses to give her what she wants, she will happily sink the boat with everyone on board.

Orgol. This Div fights with Chemosh continually for the rights of the souls of the Div-Tieflings that come to him. Orgol will fight anyone that chooses to oppose her. Due to her militant attitude about the dead, she has often fought entire wars in the infernal realm to exert her rule.

Yktat. A mostly solemn Div who prefers to stay locked away in dusty infernal libraries studying the ancient texts left by unknown lords of Hell. He does not try to get involved in the affairs of other Div lords. He mostly does not care he just wants his followers to find out information and send it to him.

Z'zbip. A mostly playful Div who likes to use the forces of nature and storms to play pranks on other infernal beings. He does not ask much of those around him, he just wants to amuse himself and those that get his attention. Unfortunately, those that get his attention usually meet their watery ends.

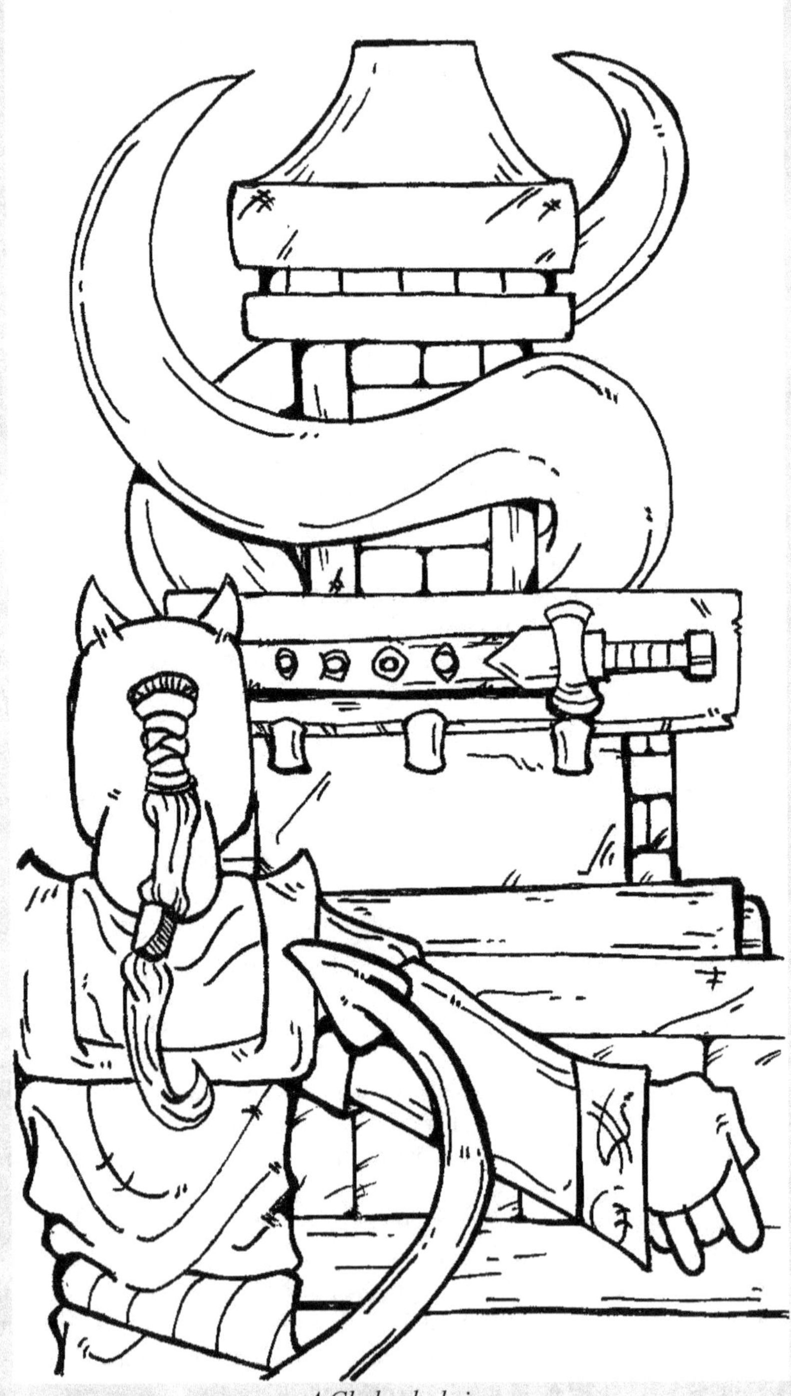

A Chalmek shrine

Adventurers

Many Div-Tieflings find great excitement in the life of an adventurer. They do not try to avoid this lifestyle as they believe it builds strength and character. Since their culture is so determined to prove dominance over others, the easiest way to do that is to show their strength in the world around them. Those that can prove they are worthy warriors are more likely to be given posts of command in kingdoms that they will often later seek to take over for themselves.

Unfortunately, the adventuring life does not always bode well for the Div-Tiefling. They often die and get seriously injured carrying out their desires. The Tieflings that fall in the adventuring life are disdained and treated with contempt by others. To come back with a grievous injury would be a great insult to other Div-Tieflings. This is a sign of weakness and that this person was not a worthy candidate for the greatness that these people are supposed to achieve.

Div-Tiefling Names

The names for these people are not wholly unlike the names of their parent races. Parents of Div-Tieflings will usually name them after some grand person of their family or nation, or else something damning when seeing the horns and tail of their child.

This does not stop the Tiefling themselves from changing their name when they come of age. It is common for the Div-Tieflings to do so. Most of them figure that they have no physical resemblance to their parents so why should they be named like them? Many of them will research other famous members of their genetics or else take the name of one of the great infernal Divs themselves. These names will often strike fear in all they encounter as a changed name to something infernal is not a good sign for the group these Tieflings have just encountered.

Div-Tiefling Traits

Div-Tieflings share certain racial traits because of their infernal descent.

Ability Score Increase. Your Strength score increases by 1, and your Charisma score increases by 2.

Age. Div-Tieflings mature at the same rate as humans but live a few years longer.

Alignment. Div-Tieflings might have an innate tendency toward evil, and many of them end up there. Evil or not, an independent nature inclines many Div-Tieflings toward a neutral alignment.

Size. Div-Tieflings are about the same size and build as humans. Your size is Medium.

Speed. Your base walking speed is 30 feet.

Darkvision. Thanks to your infernal heritage, you have superior vision in dark and dim conditions. You can see in dim light within 60 feet of you as if it were bright light, and in darkness as if it were dim light.

You cannot discern colour in darkness, only shades of gray.

Hellish Resistance. You have resistance to fire damage.

Infernal Legacy. You know the *fire bolt* cantrip. This cantrip gets stronger at a rate equal to ½ your character level. When you reach 3rd level, you can cast the *detect magic* spell as a 2nd level spell once with this trait and regain the ability to do so when you finish a long rest. When you reach 5th level, you can cast the *invisibility* spell as a 3rd level spell once with this trait and regain the ability to do so when you finish a long rest. Charisma is your spellcasting ability for these spells.

Languages. You can speak, read, and write Common and Infernal.

Variant Div-Tiefling Abilities

Not all Div-Tieflings are born with the same features. While the racial traits listed above represent the most common of Div-Tieflings, some are born with other traits that are uncommon. A gamemaster may allow a Div-Tiefling PC to either roll on the table below, or else allow them to pick one to their suiting. It may not be a good idea to let players roll on the table as it may ruin the character or class idea they may have in the forefront of their mind. However, the gods are not always friendly when determining anyone's destiny.

All the below abilities replace the Tieflings ***Hellish Resistance*** trait. Other Tieflings from other publications may also use the chart below.

Variant Div-Tiefling Ability Table

2d20	*Ability*
2	Add +1 to the Strength ability.
3	Add Thunder resistance.
4	Add advantage to Charm effects.
5	Add proficiency in Stealth.
6	Add a 1d4 damage claw attack.
7	Add Acid resistance.
8	Add +5 feet to Speed.
9	Add +1 to the Dexterity ability.
10	Add advantage to Fear effects.
11	Add Radiant resistance.
12	Add proficiency in Perception.
13	Add a 1d4 damage horn attack.
14	Add advantage to Sleep effects.
15	Add Cold resistance.
16	Add wings that gives a 20-foot fly movement. No heavy armour can be worn while flying.
17	Add +1 to the Intelligence ability.
18	Add proficiency in Survival.
19	Add Psychic resistance.
20	Add advantage to Poison effects.
21	Add a 1d4 damage poison touch attack.
22	Add proficiency in Deception.
23	Add Force resistance.
24	Add advantage to Disease effects.
25	Add +1 to the Charisma ability.
26	Add the ability to make Stealth checks at normal speed with no penalty.

27	Add Poison resistance.
28	Add a 1d4 damage fire touch attack.
29	Add advantage to Exhaustion effects.
30	Add proficiency in Sleight of Hand.
31	Add Lightning resistance.
32	Add ability to move from a blazing fire to another blazing fire as a Move action.
33	Add +1 to the Wisdom ability.
34	Add advantage to Curse effects.
35	Add Necrotic resistance.
36	Add proficiency in Persuasion.
37	Add a 1d4 damage necrotic touch attack.
38	Add advantage to Confusion effects.
39	Add Fire immunity.
40	Add immunity to all magic. Cannot cast spells. May use potions as normal.

Chapter II - New Backgrounds

Here is presented new backgrounds that can be appropriate for Div-Tieflings to take. Of course, any character can also take these backgrounds as they can be used for anyone that fits the character type that a player may desire to play.

Shunned Child

Not all children are accepted as some would prefer. There are children that are sometimes left out in the open to die as parents will not desire the child to have anything to do with the rest of their children. Sometimes this is for reasons of inheritance, deformity, bastardization or some other reason that causes the parents to want to have nothing to do with the child. Some cultures openly accept this practice, while in others it is frowned upon.

Cultures that practice this in any way, will also have people that will save these children and try to raise them in a stable home. These children still feel as outsiders and may lash out against their adoptive families, entering lives of crime or vagrancy. These children always suspect those around them as not wanting them. Others just distance themselves naturally because they have always felt they have no place with others. Many suffer from arrogance or on the other side, complete inadequacy as they try to prove their worth beyond what is normal.

Skill Proficiencies: Deception, Sleight of Hand
Tool Proficiencies: one set of Artisan's Tools, Thieves Tools
Equipment: Thieves tools, dagger, a list of 1d4 names that owe you 3d6 gp a piece, a note owing you a favour from a notable personality, stealth cloak, a guild invitation and a small pouch containing 5 gp.

Feature: Underworld Contacts

The character has contacts to different aspects of the criminal underworld. This does not mean that they know the names or secret identities of these contacts, but they do know how to leave messages or get a hold of black-market items that no one can get their hands on legally. Many authorities try to use them, willingly or not, to get into contact with these people, but they are aware that these law enforcement officers are closely watching them, making them more cautious when they leave requests with their contacts.

Suggested Characteristics

Shunned Children are private individuals who do not want to interact with most other people. Secretly they desire to be included with others, but they have a great deal of fear of letting others in. Many of them are highly introverted, but some have taken these fears and decided to face them directly. This makes these characters likely to be loud and outspoken. It is hard to tell which characters have suffered from this type of upbringing since some have embraced it while others have gone into self-imposed exile to avoid social rejection.

d8	*Personality Trait*
1	I prefer to be by myself. I do not like socializing with others as I simply do not trust them.
2	I love being the centre of attention. It makes me feel as though I am not as shunned as I was raised.
3	I take out my frustration on others. I know they are not to blame, but I still feel they are.
4	I try to forgive others for what they have done. I do not want my past to affect those around me.
5	I desire the acceptance of others and will do almost anything to get their approval.
6	I beg for others to forgive me for what I have done, even if I have not done anything wrong.
7	I do not trust anyone, and secretly seek a reason to betray them and leave them behind.
8	I have forgiven my parents, but I will never allow someone to shun me again without repercussions.

d6	*Ideal*
1	**Forgiveness.** I desire to be forgiven for wrongs in my childhood. (Lawful)
2	**Improvement.** I desire to improve society so that others do not have to suffer what I have. (Good)
3	**Revenge.** I want to pay back those that have done me wrong. (Evil)
4	**Freedom.** I believe life is short and I will do what I want to enjoy it. (Chaotic)
5	**Disinterest.** The world at large does not interest me. I just want to be left alone. (Neutral)
6	**Secrecy.** My life is my own and no one has any business in it. (Any)

d6	*Bond*
1	Those I can trust deserve my loyalty.
2	My family threw me away, I have found a new one.
3	Friends are good, I need companions.
4	I need to learn to forgive my friends.
5	Others will wrong me, and I will prove it.
6	I desire to reconcile with those that turn me away.

Starlet

A young performer that has visions of grandeur about their future. This young person does everything they can to make a point of being noticed. Other people within the community have all noticed the character and taken note of how great a performer the character is. Unfortunately, life sometimes takes a different route, and the performer needs to take a different role in life. This has usually been to the detriment of their career and the fan base.

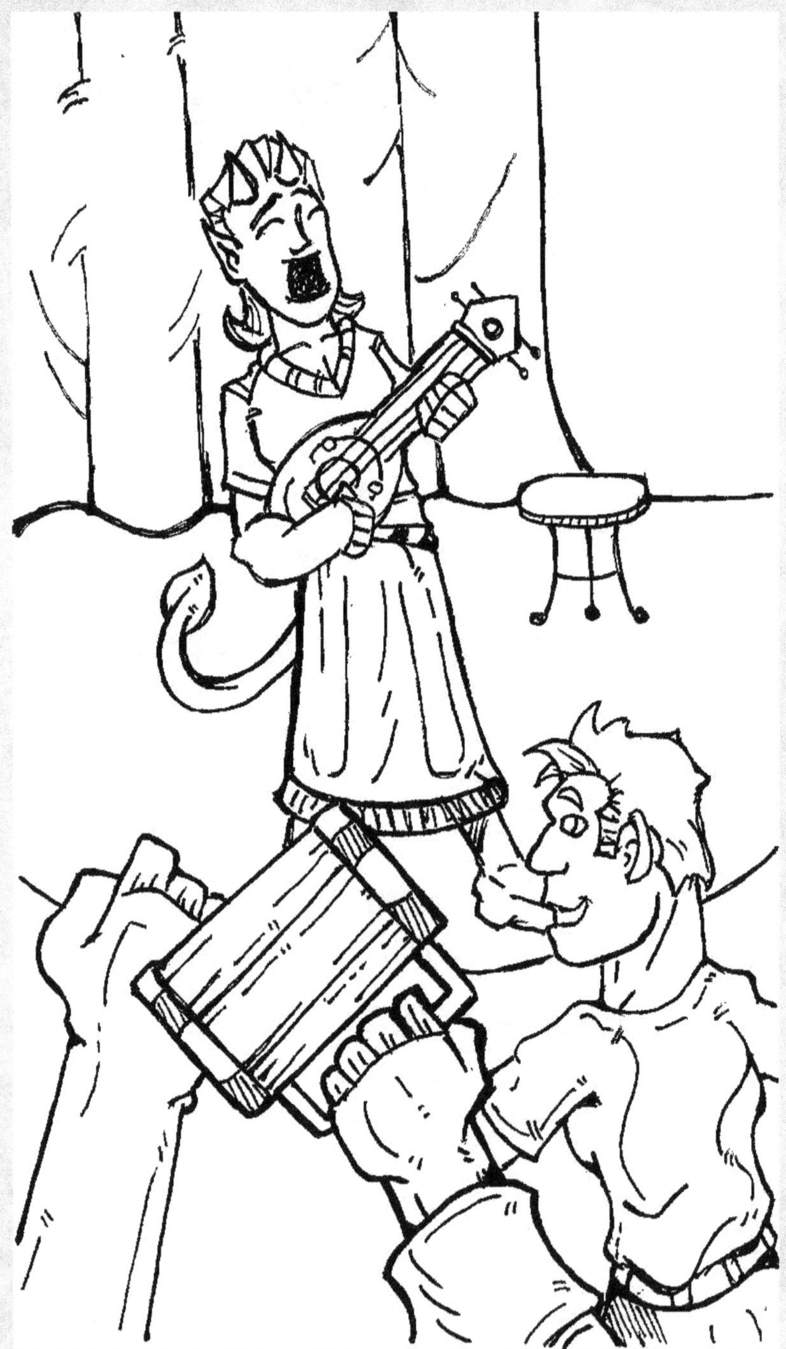

A Div-Tiefling starlet

Many people would pay great money to spend personal time with these starlets, but most never get the chance. When the adventuring life makes an often, grisly call, the starlet will usually have no choice but to respond. Some adventuring groups have found these members of their teams greatly beneficial. They have access to people that most others do not, and information tends to come to them more easily than others.

Skill Proficiencies: Insight, Performance
Languages: Two of your choice
Equipment: Makeup kit, a set of fancy clothes, a set of costumes, two favours from nobles, a stage prop and a pouch containing 2d4 gp.

Feature: Visible Personality

The character can get access to usually closed places: live performances, special dinners, notable tournaments etc. This access most times will show up as an anonymous invitation appearing out of nowhere. The starlet will usually realize that these invites come from someone that is trying to gain their favour, but these personalities will not reveal themselves until the actual event. This revealing can often create an incident among certain people at the event as the starlet is also usually known for taking their adventuring party with them.

Suggested Characteristics

Quite often the character is charming. This charm has spread to the community around them. People will try to come to meet the character for signatures or other blessings. The character may be outwardly charming, but in secret they could also be quiet and timid. This does not always define all starlets, but a vast majority of them prefer to keep their private lives private. They will normally abhor those that try to pry into personal affairs, making them keep certain people at a distance that can normally be trusted.

d8	*Personality Trait*
1	I enjoy the public attention it makes me feel welcome and wanted. Some privacy is nice, but mostly I like being the centre of attention.
2	I prefer to be on my own. I am charming externally only because people expect me to be.
3	I have a mission in life and all the things I have accomplished up until now are meaningless. I feel lost and without purpose.
4	I was once famous I am not anymore. People need to learn to mind their own business or get me angry.
5	This life will not last forever. Once I am done with the calling to adventure, I will hopefully be able to get back to my life as a performer.
6	I trust people too easily. This makes people try to take advantage of me and often leaves me openly hurt.
7	I never wanted this life, but it chose me. I must live up to the expectations that other have put on me.
8	My call to adventure has put a great weight on my soul. As result I just want to part and have a good time until my inevitable death.

d6	Ideal
1	**Mission.** I must fulfill the calling put before me to find some peace in this life. (Good)
2	**Careless.** I know I am to fulfill some great role in life, but I simply do not care. Come what may. (Neutral)
3	**Opportunity.** I want to adventure because it will offer me new opportunities in the future when I am finished this life. (Chaos)
4	**Duty.** I will do what I must. I am not sure what that may all entail, but hopefully I can fulfill my role. (Any)
5	**Privacy.** Others simply need to leave me alone. I will not impede on others to make their own choices, as long as they do the same for me. (Chaotic)
6	**Inspiration.** I am going on this journey to gain inspiration for future acts. I want to create with all that I will see and experience. (Any)

d6	Bond
1	The others are here for my amusement.
2	I feel a connection to the others that makes me loyal to them.
3	Once I am done with this journey, the others are best without me.
4	I want to develop deeper friendships with those around me.
5	I want to be noticed by someone who will make life easier.
6	The others around me need to relax and learn to have fun with me.

Chapter III - New Class Options

In this chapter are offered some new class options that may be suited for a Div-Tiefling type of character. These class options, the College of Seduction and the Usurper are perfectly representative of the type of ways that these Tieflings will get to the top of the organizations and cities they tend to take over.

Of course, both these options are also suited for other characters that want to try them. Characters could possibly have been raised in shady situations or else have been given a noble title from their family and become notable military leaders in the process. The gamemaster and player are encouraged to develop a backstory that fits perfectly into the campaign that is laid out before the characters.

New Bard College

Below is a new Bardic College available to players at the permission of the gamemaster. Not all campaigns will be appropriate for this type of character, but there will always be opportunities for a character of this college to shine if played properly.

College of Seduction

The most charming people are always the centre of attention with often hidden agendas that they rarely tell anyone. The College of Seduction actively seeks to enlist these charming individuals to attempt to learn things that no one else was ever meant to know. Some of these people readily accept the invitation, others do not.

Those that are welcomed into the college are treated like stars who have reached the zenith of their soon to come careers. These members do not always use intimate means to seduce people, but this has not been out of the realm of possibility for these college alumni. Others have used music, poetry, art, or many other ways to get their fingers (or claws) into those that their college tells them to target.

The college is very demanding in the targets they command their members to go after. There is not much option for the alumni when the college gives an order. Many times, those that do, become victims of other secretive colleges that many others do not know about. This fear of retribution by their college has caused many to not question their commands.

Performance Advantage

When you join the College of Seduction at 3rd level, you gain advantage to Charisma (Performance) checks against those of your sexual orientation.

Circle of Awe

Also, at 3rd level you gain the ability to convince others not to take violent actions against you or your allies in combat. When you spend a Bardic Inspiration die, you can make a Charisma (Persuasion) check with the bonus die added to one total check against all enemy creatures within 20 feet. If you succeed, your allies gain advantage against the creatures for up to a number of rounds equal to your Charisma modifier. Also, the enemies gain disadvantage against you and your allies until they either hit or are attacked. This feature also ends if you or an ally makes a successful attack against an individual creature. The feature remains against any creatures that are not successfully attacked for the duration.

Secrets Revealed

Starting at 6th level, you gain advantage on any two Intelligence based skills any time you are required to make a check.

Master Manipulator

At 14th level, you can spend a Bardic Inspiration die to add the die bonus and also double the ability modifier bonus on any mind-affecting spell of your choice. Also, the spell that you use this feature on lasts for twice the length that is described in the spell itself.

New Fighter Martial Archetype

This fighter archetype is based around the use of Charisma as an offensive weapon. The ability to charm and to use words as weapons has always been the key to winning almost any war or rebellion. The Usurper excels in all these areas and can be quite a menace on the battlefield.

Usurper

Desiring to overthrow a government or other type of organization, the Usurper will work their way into positions of power. They are master manipulators and combatants. Many have either a healthy respect or fear for the talents the Usurper shows both on and off the battlefield. This causes many "friends" to always approach them carefully.

The Usurper fully believes that power corrupts. That is why they want it. Someone has been corrupted by it, or else they want it because they are corrupt at heart. Both types of revolutionaries take up the call of the Usurper. Some just want to see nations burn around them, while others are trying to make a positive change. The Usurper themselves will never reveal what their true intent is since that could jeopardize their mission.

Patience is also key to their mission. The Usurper is willing to wait for years, if necessary, to make their move. Getting the trust of the nobles or commanders of the army is important. Without their support, the revolution will fail. These allies will often tread carefully around the Usurper not knowing whether their plans are for good or evil.

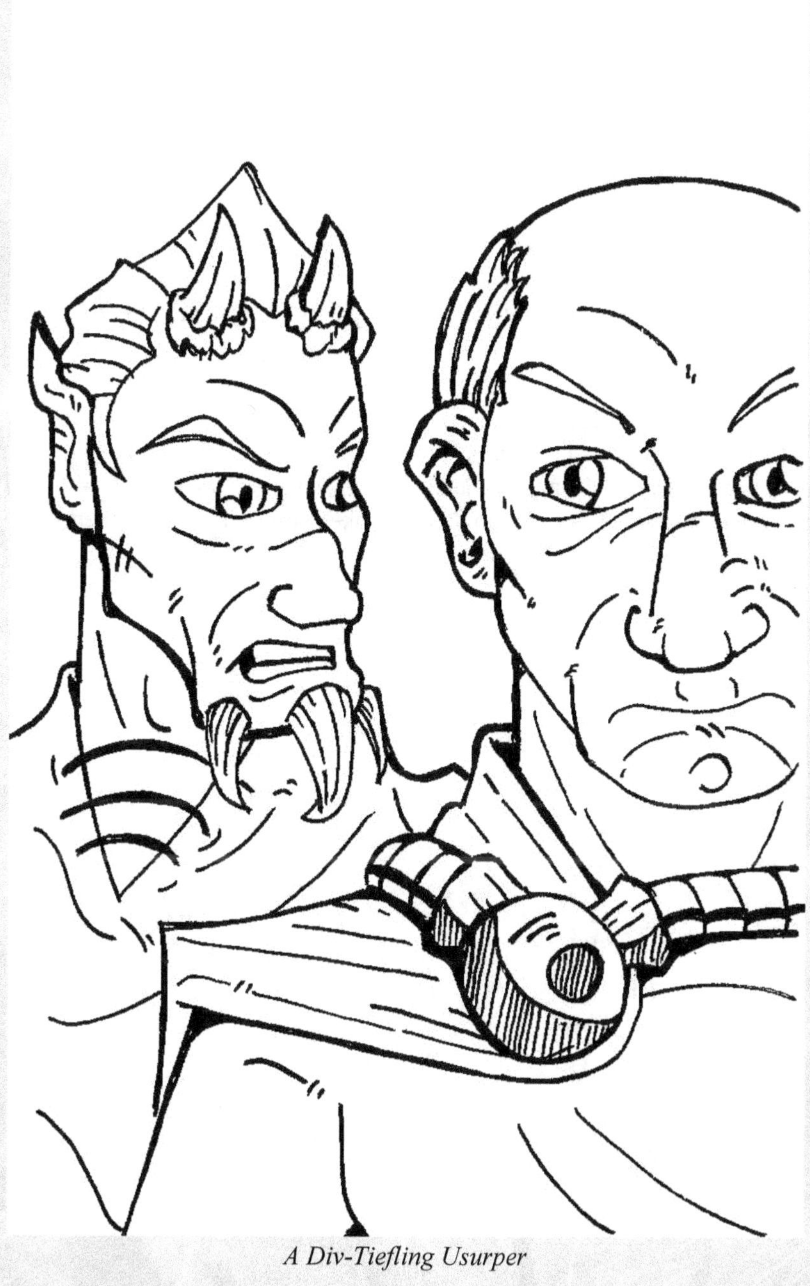

A Div-Tiefling Usurper

Bonus Proficiencies

Beginning when you choose this archetype at 3rd level, you gain proficiency in Dexterity (Acrobatics) and Intelligence (History). You also gain proficiency in Charisma saves.

Strength of the Usurper

Starting at 7th level, you can add your Strength modifier to any Dexterity (Acrobatics) and Intelligence (History) checks.

The Charismatic Rebel

Upon reaching 10th level, the Usurper may add up to half their Charisma modifier (minimum +1) to their AC.

Well Spoken Sword

When you reach 15th level you can add your Charisma modifier (minimum +1) to your weapon damage rolls.

Charmed by Strength

At 20th level, you can use your Strength modifier in place of any Charisma based skills. Also, you gain proficiency and advantage in two Charisma skills of your choice whenever you are required to make a test in the two selected skills.

Chapter IV - 4th Militia Military Camp

The 4th militia is the main military force of the Londorian Kingdom. This kingdom is a predominantly human realm that has been open to other races for many years. Recent movements within the royal court have made some hesitant to accept too many new people into the realm, but the brave courage of Queen Guendaleir has put some of these fears to rest. The current queen is confident that these new peoples will help strengthen the cultural aspects of the kingdom while also spreading good will to those in need.

What she does not realize, however, is that there are movements within the military that are trying to overthrow this noble policy. These military leaders are afraid of races like the drow or duergar who are very military minded and may take the good nature of the kingdom's monarch to infiltrate the realm. While the queen is aware of some of these anarchists, she has done little to find out exactly who is involved. Guendaleir fears that she may have to imprison some of her closest advisors if she were to unmask the plot. A time is coming however when her hand will be forced.

Her concerns may come true sooner than she had feared. The most powerful military force in the kingdom, the 4th militia, is being influenced by a Div-Tiefling that is trying to convince the general of the militia to go along with the xenophobic policies. The Tiefling is mostly unknown to the queen, thinking him a lowly lieutenant but really a close confidant of the general. It makes the situation tenuous because some of the others within the camp believe that the "robed man" (as they know him) has secret plans and is looking to destabilize the kingdom. If the throne was aware of the influence of the Div-Tiefling, she may bring him up on charges to keep the peace within the different cultures within Londorian.

The militia itself is comprised of approximately 5,000 soldiers. Most of them are human, but about 30% are dragonborn while about 5% are half-orcs. There are other races present within the military camp, but they make up only a fraction of the forces that it is difficult to give exact numbers. Due to the influence of the Tiefling, the dragonborn and half-orcs have been put into their own divisions and squads. This has caused some strife within these groups, but the desire to intermix the cultures has only met with resistance from the top of the militia's hierarchy.

About two hundred of the camps personnel are officers of the rank of captain or major. Most of the others are either sergeants, corporals, or non-ranked soldiers. There is little movement within the ranks as many of the ranking officers and non-commissioned officers act more like cowards on the battlefield than like true leaders. This causes some strife within the rank-and-file troops, but to say anything might bring up charges against these people. While the queen might be apt to give these soldiers a pardon for such action, she is also trying to maintain the peace among the armies' larger leadership. This causes her to allow generals to command their troops as they see fit. This might force some of the troops at some time to start whistle blowing to the royal court about what kind of policies the commander is enacting. As of right now, the troops are afraid. The Div-Tiefling knows this and keeps them afraid so that they will not cause any problems.

The militia is currently camped on the outskirts of the Suzerian Jungle. This jungle is right on the borders of the Londorian kingdom and brings many problems with it. Lizardfolk and Troglodytes have consistently caused problems. While the Lizardfolk have mostly kept the peace in the last few months, their war with the Troglodytes has caused some skirmishes to spill over into the kingdom proper. The 4th militia has been stationed to try and keep these conflicts within the jungle borders. Guendaleir desires that the two sub-nations of Suzerian keep it to themselves and keep the kingdom of Londorian out of the larger conflict.

Areas Within the Camp

Below are listed various areas within the military camp. These areas can be used for adventurers to interact with some NPC's or gain some equipment and information before branching off into a larger adventure. There is also the option of exposing the plot within the camps leadership. This would make for a larger campaign, but this camp could be the starting point for such a quest.

Soldiers Tents

Most of the camp is made up of hundreds of tents that typically hold ten soldiers each. These tents are large and typically bottomless, with dirt floors from constant use. The occasional tent may have sheep skin on the ground making it more comfortable, but these are rare. Many common soldiers do not have the income to live in any kind of luxury.

Many of the tents are grouped into blocks of about one-hundred soldiers each with a separate tent for the officers of the company. These companies have a common fire pit where many of the soldiers will gather throughout the day and night while other duties do not consume their time. Barrels of ale can usually be found in these areas, as well as games of chance, tables of food or other implements for the comfort and entertainment of that specific company.

For anyone trying to sneak into the camp, the Passive Perception of the soldiers is 12. Anyone that can manage to sneak into the camp can try to gain information from the troops. Usually overhearing their conversations is the best way to do this but even if they are seen, the adventurers may not even be questioned as it is not all that strange for outsiders to be in the camp. Only when the camp is in current conflict are any outsiders forbidden within the confines.

There is often a lot of loose equipment and other common military goods laying around. Many of the troops really could not care about the equipment making them lazy about keeping watch over their company area. Various illegal activities can be found happening within each company. These acts can be small things such as petty theft to large things like arson or murder.

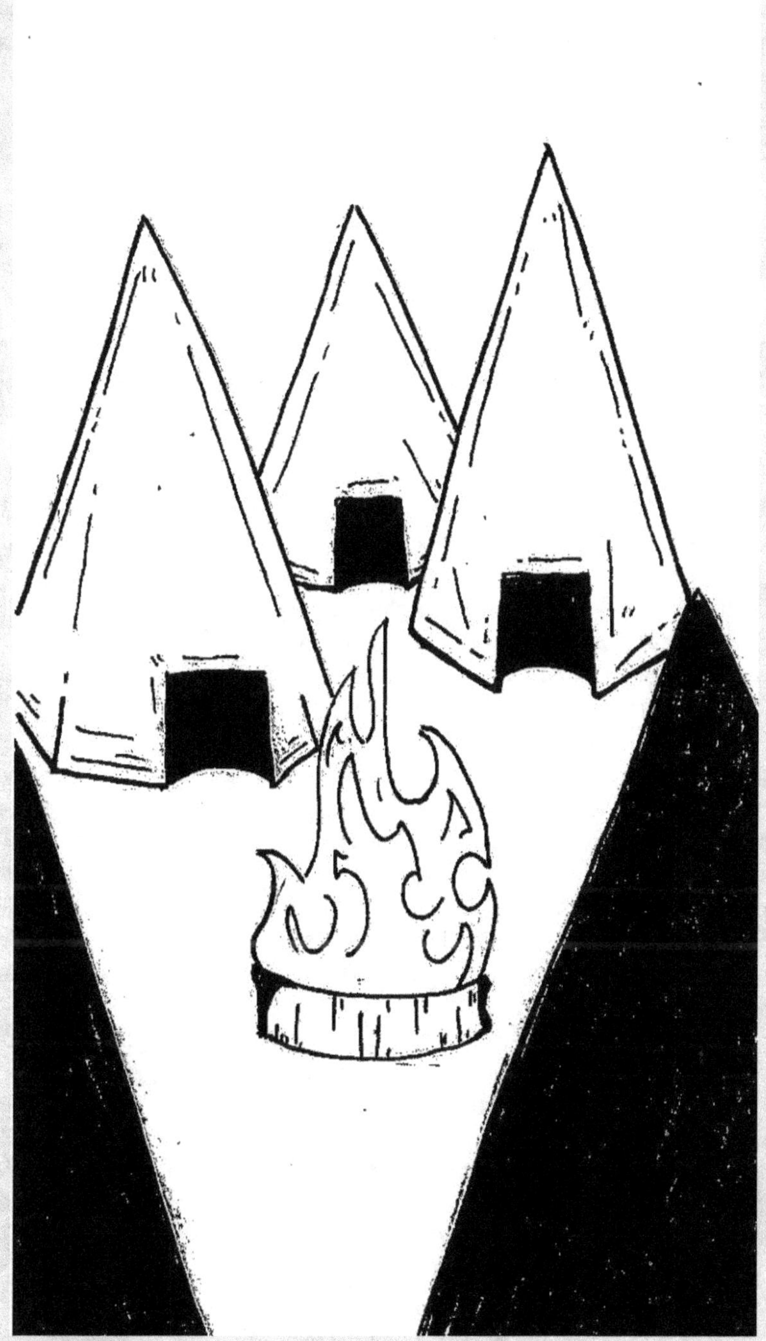

4th Militia Soldier Tents

Other soldiers may be disgruntled enough to want to hire some civilians to pull pranks or do something destructive in another area of the camp. Sometimes these are against soldiers of their own companies, but most times these jobs involve other companies that are rivals or have some goods that the hiring company wants for themselves. Rarely these jobs may be even more sinister in that a hated officer needs to be killed and the insurrectionist soldiers are not willing to do the job themselves.

Training Pits

A popular area for the soldiers to gather are the training pits. These pits are dirty and often riddled with disease, but many soldiers come here, not to train, but to challenge each other in feats of strength. When the militia is not active with fighting off Lizardfolk or Troglodyte attacks, the camp can become boring. This made it necessary for the general to form an area where the soldiers could compete with one another for entertainment. While most card or gambling competitive games are held within the companies themselves, the games with weapons are held in the training pits.

The area was given the name to hide what it primarily is, a death pit. Many soldiers have fought each other here and died. While the general is saddened by such losses, he also sees them as necessary to maintain morale. For those that do not wish to kill their own militiamen, gladiators from various regions are brought in for the soldiers to fight. These pit fights are then bet on. Most of the gladiators are slaves that have been paid for by the officers to entertain the troops. While slavery is illegal in Londorian, it nevertheless has found a market within the 4th militia. There are other nearby kingdoms where slavery is legal that supply the slaves needed for these "training pits."

These pits are also used to exact capital punishment. If a soldier is caught doing something that would otherwise break the orders of the general, the punishments are carried out in the pits. Some are just simply flogged while their fellow soldiers cheer each crack of the whip. Other more serious offences are carried out by giving the offender a club and having them fight a group of up to five others who mercilessly kill the offending soldier. These are popular events that soldiers will often fight each other outside of the training pits for the chance to witness.

At times entire groups of innocent families, including children, are bought by the officers for use in the training pits. Again, if someone were to find this out and bring one of them back to the capital to testify to the barbarism, it would put a quick end to the crimes being committed. No soldier has had the bravery to do so. If someone were to break the confidence of their battle-brothers, it would shatter morale and cause a great amount of distrust. This distrust would probably cause that individual to wake up with a dagger in their throat.

The Blacksmiths and Carpenters

This area is commonly busy and noisy. Many soldiers who have equipment in need of repair will spend a great amount of time here trying to get their gear fixed. While someone might think that the officers would bill the crown for the cost of these repairs, the general and his Div-Tiefling confidant have billed the throne for the cost but keep half the money and demanded that the soldiers pay the other half. This is part of the reason the soldiers are disgruntled and would make the queen very unhappy if she were to find out. The blacksmiths and carpenters do not care, as they will not work if they are not paid upfront. Too many officers have taken advantage of the skilled workers good-will and they are tired of it.

Luckily, the work being done here is not overpriced. It is fair work for a fair price. Some of the soldiers have tried to bargain the price down and again the workers are tired of it. They understand the situation the soldiers are in, but the equipment to make the repairs does not come free and many of the skilled workers have families they need to support.

Replacement weapons are numerous. The weapons that are produced here are of a good quality and like the prices of the repairs are fair. It is unlikely that anyone would be able to convince the blacksmiths and carpenters to sell for less, but it can be tried (DC 22). If a character is a member of the militia, then the officers will cover half the cost of the weapon, but only if it is replacing one they had before. The camp will not hand over money to buy new equipment at anyone's whim. Application can be made to acquire new weapons, but these are rarely granted.

Any character that engages in conversation with the workers will find out that someone has been stealing weapons from their stores. This does not happen frequently, but every couple of months each of the blacksmiths and carpenters will say that steel swords, bows or arrows will go missing. The general is not interested in paying for stolen items. He will not even give the workers that half that usually gets covered by their coffers. The workers have formed a guild to try and fend off the thieves, but so far there has been no success. Anyone that finds out who is doing the crimes will be rewarded with 3d6x10 gp.

Officer's Tents

This is the heart of the 4th militia. All major decisions are made here. The area is quite large as it holds the formal administrative tent as well as a small parade square where one company of the militia stand guard. Around the main tent are the officer tents, the most exquisite of which is the generals tent. The generals' tent is almost as large as the administrative tent which the commander of the camp barely ever leaves. Many servants and subordinate officers can be seen going in and out of the generals tent at all times of day, but anyone that disturbs him after sunset is in for trouble, usually in the form of a flogging.

What is suspicious is a small one-person tent that sits directly beside the generals. Some of the soldiers have suspected that the two tents are sown together in some way, but no one has been able to confirm this. While most of the soldiers can attest to the interior of the generals' tent, no one has seen the interior of the adjacent small tent. The only person that seems to go in and out of the tent is a robed man that some have said seems to have a tail jutting out of the bottom of his cloak. Any other features have been hidden from view. Who this man is, or what his relationship with the general is, has never been discovered.

This area is in no way limited to officers and is open to any of the soldiers or visitors to the camp. Many visitors make their way into this area of the camp many of them being advisors from the royal court. Other caravans also make their way directly here to drop off gold and other equipment that cannot be made by the blacksmiths and carpenters that call the camp home. A large road has been formed to allow the easy access to the administrative tent for these caravans.

A lot of illegal activity happens in this area of the camp. Any characters that can sneak into the area can at most times easily find someone scheming in the shadows of the tents. Schemes can range from theft of some of the government money, stealing plans from the generals' tent, finding compromising information from the administrative tent, or even assassinations of certain officers. Which scheme takes root to reality is hard to say. Many different plots are planned every day. Most of these schemes do not find themselves being played out because of fear of the general and that strange-robed man. This fear makes many people cancel the plan at the last minute.

Other strange things tend to happen around the officer's tents. Some have theorized that magical experiments take place in some of the tents. Some of the tents are more heavily guarded than others, the soldiers standing watch not knowing exactly what happens within. The strange-robed man is known to also come into a few of these tents and the air around tends to be charged with energy after he leaves. It would be easier to find out what was happening in the tents if it were all happening in one location, but since the tents are spread all over the officer's section of the camp, this becomes more difficult. Anyone who has magical aptitude and makes a DC 12 Intelligence (Arcana) check can easily detect that there is something magical happening in those tents.

The penalty for being caught trying to sneak into these tents is most severe. The general will command that the offender be taken away. Where these prisoners are taken is never known, but most have assumed that they are taken into the mysterious tents and experimented on. They are not wrong. The magical experiments being done in the tents usually destroys the victims so that there is nothing left to bury. It would be thought that the fear of these experiments would cause the soldiers to want to back off, but this is not enough of a deterrent. Many soldiers each day try to find their way, or even a look, into the secret tents. So far, no one has succeeded. What they might discover if they do succeed would cause them nightmares for rest of their lives.

The Robed Man

The greatest mystery is the robed man that walks his way around the officer's section of the camp. There has been a lot of speculation by militiamen and other officers of what exactly this man's relation to the general is, but no one knows for sure. Anyone who does know who the man is, has kept it a close secret, not wanting others to know his identity.

Not surprisingly, the man is a Div-Tiefling that is trying to get complete control of the camp. The Tieflings name is Taryn Vayne, the son of two human parents in the capital of Londorian. His parents had shunned him, sending him to fend for himself when his Tiefling features became too prominent to hide with baggy clothes and cloaks. These parents were nobles with a lot of influence in the royal court. While they tried to keep contact with him over the years, he has become more disdainful of them and is now seeking to take the kingdom down as a violent act against his folks. The queen herself has no idea that the Vayne's had borne a Tiefling son, she would not condemn them if she did.

The magical experiments he is undertaking are an attempt to make a super-human soldier with the strength of an orc and the speed of an elf. Vayne knows that he cannot overthrow the kingdom with the 4th militia alone. If he can manage to create a super-human-militiamen, then it would tip the scales in Vayne's favour. Every advantage he can get, he will take. Vayne's magical experiments have caused him to have contacted the realms of the Hells. These infernal lords have told him what he needs to make these experiments successful. The demons and devils have revealed that the secret lies within the Suzerian Jungle. Vayne believes it is an amulet with ancient infernal power, but even he is unsure.

How close Vayne is to discovering the secret item in the jungle is not known, but he needs the money from the general to succeed. Without that support, his ability to wage this personal war will soon dry up. If someone were able to expose Vayne and report him to the royal court, it could possibly save Londorian from a long, brutal civil war.

Taryn Vayne

Medium humanoid (div-tiefling), neutral evil

Armour Class: 15 (leather armour, arcane protection)
Hit Points: 132 (24d8 + 24)
Speed: 30 feet

Str	*Dex*	*Con*	*Int*	*Wis*	*Cha*
11 (+0)	13 (+1)	12 (+1)	16 (+3)	14 (+2)	19 (+4)

Skills: Arcana +6, Deception +7, Perception +5, Persuasion +7
Senses: Darkvision 60 feet, passive Perception 15
Languages: Common, Infernal
Challenge: 5 (1,800 XP)

Innate Spell Casting: Vayne's innate spell casting ability is Charisma (spell save DC 15). He can innately cast the following spells, requiring no material components:

At will: *fire bolt (counts as level 3 proficiency)*
1/day each: *detect magic, invisibility*

Spell Casting: Vayne is a 6th level spell caster. His spell casting ability is Charisma (spell save DC 15, +7 to hit with spell attacks). He has the following sorcerer spells prepared:

Cantrips (at will): *Acid Splash, Chill Touch, Mage Hand, Minor Illusion, True Strike*

1st level (4 slots): *Burning Hands, Charm Person, Disguise Self, Magic Missile*

2nd level (3 slots): *Alter Self, Hold Person, Suggestion*

3rd level (3 slots): *Blink, Fireball, Protection from Energy*

Actions

Multiattack: Vayne makes 6 shortsword attacks.

Shortsword: *Melee Weapon Attack:* +4 to hit, reach 5 feet, one target. *Hit:* 5 (1d6 + 1) piercing damage.

Arcane Strike: *Melee Weapon Attack:* +8 to hit, reach 5 feet, one target. *Hit:* 32 (8d6 + 4) magic damage.

OPEN GAME LICENSE Version 1.0a

www.ingramcontent.com/pod-product-compliance
Lightning Source LLC
LaVergne TN
LVHW010549100826
845148LV00013B/2673